NO KNOWN COORDINATES

Also by Maria Terrone:

The Bodies We Were Loaned
A Secret Room in Fall
American Gothic: Take 2
Eye to Eye
Life, Death, & Cash
At Home in the New World

NO KNOWN COORDINATES

Maria Terrone

THE WORD WORKS
Celebrating 50 Years

No Known Coordinates © 2025 Maria Terrone

Reproduction of any part of this book in any form
or by any means, electronic or mechanical,
except when quoted in part for the
purpose of review, must be
with permission in writing
from the publisher.
Address inquiries
directly to:

THE WORD WORKS
P.O. Box 42164
Washington, D.C. 20015
editor@wordworksbooks.org

No part of this book may be used
or reproduced in any manner
for the purpose of training
artificial intelligence
technologies
or systems.
Ever.

Author photograph: William Terrone
Cover design: Susan Pearce
Cover art: Image by Frances Coch,
rights purchased from iStock.

ISBN: 978-1-944585-85-3

Acknowledgments

I am grateful to the editors of the following publications where these poems were first published, some with slightly different wording.

The Common: "Under the El," "Bird Man," "New Wave: Post Op," "Under the Hawthorn," "The Children's Wing"
Cream City Review: "Erased"
Escape Into Life: "Snow Has Taped Shut the Loud Mouth of My City," "Two Meetings"
Hospital Drive: "Scratching the Surface," "Message to Google Earth"
The Hudson Review: "Edgar Allan Poe Dines With Thomas Jefferson," "The White Piano," "Maple Tree in Late October Beyond a White Screen," "Handbag," "Your blood was no longer on the stone," "Of Tattoos and Medieval Messages," "Galilee"
The Ilanot Review: "The Cage"
I-70 Review: "Pigeons," "What We Wear in the Subway," "Hell Gate," "Hall of Mirrors"
Literal Latté: "Closed for Now"
Ocean State Review: "Disappearing Act"
Ovunque Siamo: New Italian-American Writing: "City Hawk," "The Blank Billboard," "Miss Revlon," "Rain," "On New Year's Eve"
The Paterson Literary Review: "Jaipur Wedding Palace, Queens," "Comic Book Man," "Locks," "The Parking Lot"
Pirene's Fountain: "Sonnet After the Fall," "The Birthday Gift"
Poet Lore: "The Classification Unit"
Presence: "A Theft," "At a Vertical Tour," "Consider Her Green Dress"
Quiddity: "Reversals"
Slant: "In the Sculpture Garden"
Tar River Poetry: "The Gun," "Glimpsed"
2 Bridges Review: "Erased From the Permanent Record," "All Day the Snow Fell"
Valparaiso Poetry Review: "Nearly Blind Now, My Mother Is Having Visions," "Speaking in Tongues"
VIA: "Flowers Dark & Light," "The Notebooks"
Willow Review: "A Girl in Winter," "In Pursuit of Black," "Not an Autumn Elegy," "Mother's Confession," "Young Heritage, Inc."

"Your blood was no longer on the stone" appears in the anthology *Stronger Than Fear: Poems of Empowerment, Compassion, and Social Justice* (Cave Moon Press, 2022).

"Rain" was nominated for a 2019 Pushcart Prize by *Ovunque Siamo: New Italian-American Writing*.

"A Girl in Winter," "Mother's Confession," "Young Heritage, Inc.," and "In Pursuit of Black" were *Willow Review* award winners in 2015, 2019, 2022, and 2024 respectively.

Special Thanks

I am deeply grateful to many editors, writers, friends, and family who've supported me and my work, some recently, others for decades. Among them are Eamon Grennan and Enid Shomer, my extraordinary poetry mentors who helped me develop my voice as a writer. I also thank Dana Gioia, Anthony and Maria Tamburri, Paula Deitz, John Hennessy, Rhina Espaillat, Gerry LaFemina, Daniela Gioseffi, Michael Palma, Paul Mariani, Marie DiRocco, Chistine and Frank Lombardi, Nancy Mannion, Joanna Vasquez, Bob Rotondi, Ron Farina, Mary Lou Edmundson, Paola Corso, Mary Ann Miller, Marisa Frasca, Peter Covino, Joanna Clapps Herman, Maria Mazziotti Gillan, and many other members of the Italian American writing community. Special gratitude goes to editor Bibi Wein, whose advice was invaluable in organizing this manuscript, and always, to my husband, Bill Terrone.

I thank Nicole Cooley, Elton Glaser, and Rachel Hadas, who generously provided their wonderful blurbs for *No Known Coordinates*, and The Word Works, which published my first book in 2002 under editor Karren Alenier and this collection under editor Nancy White. I so much appreciate their ongoing enthusiasm for my work and their lifelong dedication to poetry and poets.

Contents

One: *Disappearing Acts*

    Under the El / 15
    A Theft / 16
    Nearly Blind Now, My Mother Is Having Visions / 17
    Erased From the Permanent Record / 18
    In the Sculpture Garden / 19
    Disappearing Act / 20
    Edgar Allan Poe Dines With Thomas Jefferson / 21
    Bird Man / 23
    Closed for Now / 24
    At a Vertical Tour / 25
    New Wave: Post Op / 26
    The Palace at 3 or 4 a.m. / 27
    The White Piano / 28

Two: *The Tree's True Color*

    A Girl in Winter / 31
    Reversals / 32
    In Pursuit of Black / 33
    Lost in Acres of Corn / 34
    The Source / 35
    Sonnet After the Fall / 36
    The Gun / 37
    Pigeons / 38
    Not an Autumn Elegy / 39
    Under the Hawthorn / 40
    Maple Tree in Late October Beyond a White Screen / 41
    Glimpsed / 42

Three: *Hidden City*

    Jaipur Wedding Palace, Queens / 45
    What We Wear in the Subway / 46
    All Day the Snow Fell / 47
    Flowers Dark & Light / 48
    The Birthday Gift / 49

Hell Gate / 50
City Hawk / 51
Speaking in Tongues / 52
The Blank Billboard / 53
Snow Has Taped Shut the Loud Mouth of My City / 54

Four: *Her Secrets*

Miss Revlon / 57
Handbag / 58
The Children's Wing / 59
Comic Book Man / 60
The Classification Unit / 61
Locks / 62
Mother's Confession / 63
Erased / 64
Young Heritage, Inc. / 65
Consider Her Green Dress / 66
The Notebooks / 67

Five: *No Known Coordinates*

The Cage / 71
Hall of Mirrors / 72
Your blood was no longer on the stone / 73
Rain / 75
Film Loop: Two Hotels / 77
Scratching the Surface / 78
Message to Google Earth / 79
Of Tattoos and Medieval Messages / 80
The Parking Lot / 81
Two Meetings / 82
Galilee / 83
On New Year's Eve / 84

About the Author / 87
About The Word Works / 88
Other Word Works Books / 89

For Paula Deitz

"Like a small boat adrift in the fog,
she caught glimpses during patches
when the mist cleared of a world far away,
in which everything was changing."

— Ruth Ozeki, *A Tale for the Time Being*

"Yes I know: the thread you have to keep finding, over again,
to follow it back to life…"

—Jean Valentine, "Sanctuary," from *Door in the Mountain,
New and Collected Poems, 1965-2003*

One:

Disappearing Acts

Under the El

Sun slanted down through the slats
of the elevated train onto
my fat baby hand that held
a shadow-tarnished toy, light & dark
poured out in equal measure.
From my carriage I saw

its tracks across my skin
and everywhere my gaze fell—
lamp post, cracked pavement,
the faces of strangers. I saw how light & dark
could shift into a new pattern and then
how that pattern could lift away.

I saw, without knowledge, the flux
we're born to. My mother's face
stayed hidden as she pushed me
through the East Harlem market,
my fist holding, then releasing,
its fleeting tattoo.

A Theft

Deep within the tiny shop in Rome, a woman is drawn
to the painting of a child savoring gelato in an outdoor café.
She moves closer to inspect, penetrating the clutter,
and sees her son, two decades earlier, wearing
that blue sweater she bought him there, and she sees
herself seated across the table, a mother watching
her child with indulgent pleasure, ignorant
of being seized. But by whom?
No one stood before an easel, stroking them
into another life across the canvas that she holds now
like a relic. She thinks: no, they were captured
in the era of shutter click, of a bath inside a locked,
darkened room, the stolen scene slowly
emerging. Their photo studied with a voyeur's eye,
and only then painted and framed in gold—
the color surely chosen to reflect the light.
She recalls it was late afternoon,
light soft and beginning to suffuse, before time
brought its changes. After the thief was done
with them both, then what? Yet another life
with strangers, nailed to a wall above a sofa, later sold?
Or abandoned in a storage bin, ending
in this dusty shop for how long, barely visible?
The woman knows she must reclaim the son
taken from her. Not asking the price,
she holds the painting close in both her arms.

Nearly Blind Now, My Mother Is Having Visions

Three women stood at the foot of her bed this morning,
silent when she demanded to know who they were.
For years as a child, I'd hear about the strangers
who inhabited her dreams, grim Cassandras
whispering warnings, but they've grown bolder
in my mother's tenth decade—slipping into daylight,
crossing the line. So many lines are blurred
these days: between waking and sleep, between
her hand and the white pills spilled across the table,
between my half-face and my bitten lips quivering
behind the mask. Her strained eyes flutter,
and I wish I could blink away this scene
and bring back the sight of my mother,
just returned from a flea market, inspecting her finds
with a jeweler's loop, tiny worn markings magnified
to the magnificence of 14K.
I must approach so near in order to be seen
or I'll blur, too, daughter obscured, merging with air.
The visitors return with impunity but keep their distance.

Erased From the Permanent Record

The music skipped when we hit a bump
in the road. I'd been talking but
we both stopped in the stunning silence—
me mid-sentence, she mid-song.
You kept driving, so the wheels (and earth)
must have continued to spin, and I fell back
to that meltdown of a summer
at the chemical plant when light
like no other—sudden, atomic—pierced
the high, grimy windows, struck
the chrome carriage and metal desk where
I sat, typing—a millisecond's blinding.
And deafening, too, as if
a dome had descended over me
quick as a guillotine, snuffing out
the secretaries' chatter, footfall,
even the other factories' drone.
Then clatter and motion resumed
(snap of a hidden switch) as if
what had happened didn't matter,
and so was struck from time's record.

In the Sculpture Garden

—Museum of Modern Art, NYC

Some art can make me wonder what isn't there—
this metal rose cast six times the height of a man
is surely meant to signify something other than
a bloom. And what of Calder's butterfly, a winged
whimsy of red and yellow about to take flight, alive
though born of steel? I stared at that, too,
still seeking more, then turned to face "The Back,"
a life-sized bronze relief of muscled human form
that Matisse pared down over and again to stark
abstraction: man reduced to pillar. Enter George,
a dear friend dead seven years, but standing
just yards away now, his sandy hair fading
to gray. He's middle-aged, not yet old and ill,
grinning, self-possessed as ghosts and art can be,
there for their own sake, not to answer questions.
And like this art, he doesn't notice me or say
why he is, not was, and how he came here, to be.

Disappearing Act

—After the Artist Bruce Nauman

My face against
      a train window: ghost
on glass,
        a face you can nearly
            see through,
                    dissolving
into the random
        passing landscape:

woman in field with grazing cow,

woman and abandoned mill,

woman   layered over

skyscraper, house door, lamppost.

Woman as Dadaist construct,

meant to exist   briefly,

be seen,   then disappear.

        No wonder

I want to press   my breath

between two pages of a book.

Edgar Allan Poe Dines With Thomas Jefferson

— March 1826

Couldn't he have been
among those students routinely chosen

to meet with the university founder
and discuss Enlightenment ideals?

Perhaps not. Too haunted in his bearing,
too otherworldly, too Romantic,

too poor, a Southerner but not an aristocrat
who brought his slave to school.

Still, much to praise—at 17, possessed
of a strange brilliance,

admitted early to the new university.
So picture Edgar closing the door

of Room 13, West Range—where eerie
words were whispered and roared

to wide-eyed young men before a hissing
hearth—now seated under a skylight

at the small table the Founding Father preferred.
Picture that room at Monticello—

chrome-yellow bright, of classical symmetry
that embraces order and reason, dinner prepared

by Sally Hemings' brother James, trained
as a chef in Paris during his master's stay.

What would the raven say, hovering above?
Beware the red red wine, the daggering,

deceptive crystal, this fire-flickered room,
over lit. Conversation flows.

Edgar holds his own, but there are black flashes
in his pondering and brooding in the lulls.

Possibly Jefferson notices, aware
that Edgar's father abandoned the family,

his mother dead soon after,
and that John Allan, a prosperous merchant,

disapproved of his ward, taken in
at age two but never officially adopted.

Later in the darkness that is Edgar's true home,
he steps onto the raw planks of his Spartan room,

lights a wick, dips a quill, and begins
to write "Tamerlane." Story interruptus:

by December, John Allan will refuse to pay tuition
despite the freshman's honor grades,

and Edgar will leave Charlottesville
in debt and shame:

"…it was my crime to have no one on Earth
who cared for me, or loved me,"

he wrote of that time like a doomed character
in one of his own tales,

so close that year to a future
without his raven-in-waiting.

Bird Man

> *"You were only waiting for this moment to be free."*
> —Lennon/McCartney, *"Blackbird"*

As a Bronx kid at a homeless shelter, he watched
a peregrine falcon devour a pigeon on the windowsill,

and what began in violence leapt to awe,
and awe begat beauty.

He's grown to be a birder who shares our passion.
Through the lens, he sights a warbler

and the flash of a goldfinch who's migrated North,
whispering his excitement.

And yet he remains apart, that rare species among us,
for unlike us, when alone

he must take the greatest care removing
binoculars from his backpack,

must handle them slowly, keeping them in full view
for they are black,

the color and size of a gun. Am I wrong
to think of him as a blackbird—no, a starling,

iridescent, grazing the earth at dusk and dawn
in city parks but gazing up, not down?

But he also peers into the dense
hiding places he knows well,

the shadow-cover where the living
must sometimes take refuge to stay alive.

Closed for Now

Before my travels, I rip away the magazine label
so no one will see my name, as if this useless
reflex could protect me. I carry
a cylinder of Life Savers without irony, a pen,
and my own hand, skin like parchment ready
to be inked. In the subway arcade
the barbershop is dark, a scrawled note taped
to its door: Sorry. We are closed Now.

Such gaiety in the faces of the talk show guests,
gesturing from a flat-screen TV that looms
above empty enamel chairs. Their soundless
speech fuels my sudden fear for the owner—
a Buddhist convert, I've been told, the one
who scatters carnations daily at the base
of a scrawny elm nearby. Crescents of black hair
track across the floor like commas in a narrative:
this and this and then this happened here.

But I don't know what happened here, and wonder
if "Now" is temporary or forever, a capitalized
moment that will never go beyond itself, and if
the lips will continue to move
until someone pulls the plug, and if
the message applies to me as I turn to descend
more steps that will carry me deeper down.

At a Vertical Tour

Our eager guide, no longer visible,
has ascended to heaven and I'm alone,
rear guard to a column of pilgrims,
squeezed in the tightening grip of stone
and wall. Still I climb this shaft
built for a single body's passage,
twisting round wedge-shaped stairs worn
slippery-smooth. My heart pounding
in its cloister of bone, I ache
for sunlight and vision—long to see
my future spread before me,
like a new land to explorers
who hugged the earth's curves, believing.

When sweat blurs my sight
to a single step, I picture
medieval masons heaving rock
on this spot where I labor in fear—
their faithful hearts
must have quickened, candles
against an inky sea,
their very lives chiseled
in offering. From far below,
an organ's muffled notes rise,
as if reaching for the spires
the builders knew only in fragments
but envisioned complete. Oh to see
with their perspective—
the whole, triumphant sweep
of cathedral and above, the yearning
cupola of sky.

New Wave: Post Op

Such an adrenaline rush to find
        myself alive
this seventh time, injected
        with glee on the stretcher,
making my usual "I'm o.k." calls,

and thinking I'd heard the surgeons' banter
        as I struggled to swim back up
to the light and cold,
        their talk about a French film
recently revived,

but I couldn't know for sure
        because I was a body freeze-framed,
halted in black and white
        on the grainy sand
of a beach like Antoine Doinel
trying to flee those 400 blows.

The Palace at 3 or 4 a.m.

The certificate says I was born at 2:45 a.m.,
a time for disturbances
in hotel corridors, for peepholes
and fuzzy fisheye views of lunarlike hallways,
the feeling I've landed here
from somewhere else.

At 4 a.m., I hear footfall and growls
(but no dogs are allowed here).

I rise in my white nightgown
to hover barefoot at the double-bolted door,
peering, listening.

And then the answer:

a long silence
stretched out like Giacometti figures that Sartre described
as "always mediating between nothingness and being."

And nothing to see in that hallway.

The White Piano

How it floated in the townhouse,

    whose glass façade was not a window,

but a lens through which I peered.

    How it glowed against the dark

of the other rooms, against the gloom

    of that hour, slick as a luxury ship

on the sea of winter, the bleak cold

    of a city street. How solid and yet ethereal,

as if suspended on clear thread,

    the dangled promise of another life.

I stood before it, waiting. But how still

    its bone-white fingers remained,

how relentlessly empty that room.

Two:

The Tree's True Color

A Girl in Winter

Once as a girl I lay down
in late afternoon on my bed and knew
when I awoke, cold and alone
in the upstairs room, that winter had come,
and winter had entered me.
I wore its charcoal smudge like Ash Wednesday
but not on my forehead—within,
and I was changed by that, the knowledge
a mark that would not wash off.
In one hour the bronze light had been
snuffed out, the tree outside had given up
its last leaves and now scratched
at my window. I noticed the silence
of the sparrows and the house where I lived,
a silence that covered me like a hooded robe
as if I myself were a figure of death—
but no, just a girl stepping from her bed,
winter now in the girl.

Reversals

Black bark becomes white in snow,
        the world outside this window

like a photo's negative. Time
        is just a change of perspective,

a look through a telescope's wrong end
        to then: a darkroom distorted

by distance & memory, us standing close
        together in its hush, waiting to see

what develops—all the images we seized
        for ourselves, young and rapacious.

The timer ticking in that sealed space.
        Countdown in the dark, acidic air.

Such power to know we could make
        dark eyes white holes into a vast interior,

fingernails suddenly black. We left
        the negatives hanging from their hooks,

we left the shock of our own frightful faces,
        but just for a while—like snow

before it slides away, revealing
        first a tree and then the tree's true color.

In Pursuit of Black

Queen of Night, La Tulipe Noire,
Black Hero: botanists bred them
dark darker darkest
plucking poetic names
for their creations, coming close
but never achieving true black.

Like tall night watchmen
all wearing camouflage in the last row,
they bend toward the other tulips,
solicitous over party-swaying reds
and nursery-pale pastels.

At dusk, their petals like blotters
drawing darkness to themselves,
their silent spirits hover
in the not-quite-black shadow.

Let them be benign.
Let them speak to us
when we walk together
in our own silence.

Let them tell us
the white bloom of stars
and moon is coming,
and let us believe.

Lost in Acres of Corn

Yet another video
on my computer screen.

12 hours she was missing.
Overnight.
A three-year-old and
her dog.

Towering blades
so dense
they blocked the light.

To be lost in such a story
knowing its ending:
grace and joy.

To be lost in my own story,
not knowing
who might be searching
for me in the maze.

Shall I curl up in darkness
as the child did,
and sleep?

Shall I awaken and rise
in first light
to find myself?

The Source

Lichen clings to the weathered bench
                in the hedge-encircled spot
where I sit, in retreat from last night's dreams.

First pink of a dogwood so pale against
                the early light, struggling

like all new things to be seen.
                Not yet—the blossoms
still a painter's brushstroke of becoming.

A small bird flits past, head and chest daubed
                the rosy-orange tint of dawn,

blithe spirit vanishing into a tree's cave. Warblers
                whistle complex tunes,
each green immensity harboring

a hidden chorus. This morning is a mystery
                that leaves few clues—

the breeze brushing my shoulder
                like a knowing stranger,
and that Pied Piper trail of notes I'll follow

to the source despite the distant traffic thrum—
                now, more insistent.

Sonnet After the Fall

Every skin pierce a possible intrusion,
every itch the signal of disease—
and so our lakeside idyll becomes the unease
that returns all my old suspicions.
This peace, this beauty are the illusions
of a fool. Our friends who'd visited here just called
from Emergency Care, three ticks burrowed
into their skin. Who knows where the deed was done?
Threats lie everywhere, unseen, even in my breast
as I learned nine years ago, symptomless. As my friend,
a poet and musician knew, who succumbed
at fifty-six a month ago, her music arrested
mid-song. As the carp we watched knew too late,
flapping in a raptor's claw sideways, as if on a plate.

The Gun

A child has left a yellow plastic gun
in our garden. It lies lodged
in the crook of a V formed
by the wandering
roots of a maple colossus.

The gun points due south towards
the busy avenue—a gun
only four inches long, to fit a tiny hand.
No lemon shines as bright as this barrel,
no spring leaf welcomes
like the green of its trigger.

An ant climbs over the roots' gnarled
network and within, over sparse grass,
moss, and the brittle, curled fingers
of last year's leaves,
climbs over the gun that nests, so still,
within the tree's craggy cradle.

Pigeons

Their iridescence like oil-tainted puddles
after rain, as if even their beauty
carries the stain of original sin. First birds
of my childhood, mundane as sparrows,
co-inhabitants of cracked sidewalks
and the pebble-strewn driveway behind our houses.
Reviled nuisance once revered as gods
that streaked across the skies of ancient Persia,
bearing the weight of urgent news
lightly. Monogamous. Focused. Secretive as spies.

Once from a bench near the Capitol I watched
their troops bobbing in military precision,
a back-and-forth march below sun-buffed
stairs, and wondered if they hold in their DNA
the memory of heroes—how one of their own,
wounded by gunshot, delivered a message
that saved two hundred French soldiers,
and another clocked 20 miles in 20 minutes to stop
the bombing of a village the Nazis had just left,
Allied wings on the runway, about to take flight.

Not an Autumn Elegy

Sky and clouds peek through the leaves
of this once-lush bush now riddled
with holes. Mesmerized, I gaze

from below, wondering if this fragile
yellow lace already curling to ash
could actually hold the firmament.   Imagine

a woman adrift on a life raft, eyes raised,
clinging to the hope of distant stars.
          Nearby someone has placed

a cross-section of our once-towering
maple. I wish I knew how to read these rings
encircling the dark planet at the tree's core.

Fifty years here? A hundred? Yet so smooth
on my palm and slightly damp,
as if its sap still flowed, right into my lifeline.

Under the Hawthorn

"Weeping Cherub," Durer's woodcut,
has appeared in the tree's warts
to pierce my heart, soon replaced by beasts

that cling up and down the gnarled trunk,
a fierce demon-watch over me.

I sit here to try to make sense
of some conundrum in my life,
feeling kinship with this tree, the confusion

of its history. Would-be lovers danced
around its May pole, and in ancient Greece,

brides wore crowns of white Hawthorn blooms
that Celts and Brits would later banish
from their homes, fearing doom—

the sweet, insidious enemy within.
I sit beneath this thorny tree sacred

to Druids, haven of fairies, guardian
of the spirit world, whose spiny branches
made witches' brooms, and some avow,

Christ's crown of thorns.
Tree that leans away from the weight

of its contradictions, at home
with my restless presence and dissonance
of the cognitive kind:

I hold this truth/untruth to be
self-evident/ hidden.

A centenarian, modern tree
steeped in conflicting mythologies,
daring me to touch a leaf.

Maple Tree in Late October Beyond a White Screen

It's holding fast
to its fury,

while I stare from my desk
just as a sailor, adrift
past dusk,
might fix his eyes
on a distant light.

Word by word,
this white-faced monitor
fills up,
my argument against
the void—

the pen-and-ink delicacy
of branches
soon to be weighed down
with bandages
of snow,

the long, slow erasure.

Glimpsed

Through high reeds,

through a narrow opening,

two grown egrets and seven juveniles tiptoe

through the pond's shallow waters that remain

so still, their reflections double the gathering

to eighteen members, all dressed

in baptismal white, a single arrow

of sun piercing through the trees and glancing

off their feathers. And then they stop,

while the bent branches of a birch tree

on the bank crisscross the pond so that

the egrets' gold toes seem planted

on white wood that's also a mirror of itself

meeting the birds' heads that now bow down,

beaks barely touching the water

as if held there—like this moment, our breath,

my prayer for this peace between us to last.

Three:

Hidden City

Jaipur Wedding Palace, Queens

Sometimes I'd catch the flash
of rhinestones, blinking them away
like painful dust motes as I rushed by
in my morning commute,
each store window a dreamscape
of emerald & gold:

Aladdin slippers in every size,
turbaned heads on parade,
and best of all, disembodied fingers
chained to gold-filigreed cuffs,
each side-by-side window
like a film frame unreeling a mystery.

When I stopped to admire
the Jaipur Wedding Palace display,
three child mannequins caught
my eye, nearly overshadowed
by the dazzle of their elders. How strange
they were blonde and pink-lipped as putti

and stranger still, that one in the middle,
floating in coral chiffon, was bald
as a cancer poster child.
Her blue eyes gazed within and without,
the way a lake on a clear day can hold
both the sky and its own hidden depths.

Like the flower child I was in a past life,
I heard George sing to a sitar's drone,
*And life goes on within you
and without you.* "He and the baby goddess
have all the secrets," I thought, descending
the steps into the underground.

What We Wear in the Subway

There was the high-heeled woman born male
who entered, a sandwich atop her crown, and sat
daintily, all six feet of her, military-straight,

and the man caped in a shredded garbage bag
who swept past, glaring, but didn't speak,
black plastic crackling like a slow-burning fuse,

and the nose-pierced boy with a skull-inked tee
who rose before the woman in a gold dashiki
jolted backwards by our screeching carriage,

and the traveler whose pet mouse skittered
along the pitted road of his arm, then settled,
a white fur collar nuzzling his muscled neck,

and always the health aides crumpled
at the end of the day in cartoon-printed
smocks, and the dust-coated workers

spreading their steel-toed boots who nod,
eyes shut, hands resting at last on their thighs.
And us, the passengers who hide inside the parade,

who watch our fellow passengers and then look away,
then down, down, all of us riding below the river,
wrapped in our skin-tight sheaths of silence.

All Day the Snow Fell

like people on a city street

    who do not touch, but know without

        thought that all are bound

for the same place, briefly beautiful

    in their gathering. Still they remain

apart, fiercely alone, unknown

    to one another.   All day long

        each snowflake fell, and falling ourselves

under their spell, we wondered if we should stop

    what we were doing, stop

        the fall with a camera's freeze-action—

but in the end, we moved about through our day

    and did not succumb

        to the futile urge for a simple still life.

Flowers Dark & Light

Before dawn the florist plants blooms, left over
from society events, in unlikely places—

Our newlyweds' apartment faced an alley
where no sun or people passed.

lidless garbage cans, subway exits, shuttered banks
graffiti-scarred and doused with poison.

Its gloom seeped into me
and settled like never-ending night.

Once he scattered 17,000 pink carnations,
a munificent gift for passers-by.

I don't recall placing a bouquet
in those rooms during our four-year exile.

A man dragging a battered suitcase took
a fistful of orchids from a fence and began to sing.

When the #2 train rumbled around the corner, soot
gathered at our windows like shredded petals.

The Birthday Gift

We rode the subway into Brooklyn, following the directions
from the classified ad. Only now I know
we were crossing a border. The stations had names, not
street numbers, which seemed exotic and slightly sinister.
Nearly ten, I had a dread of getting lost, and when we blinked back
the sunlight after hours underground, it was blinding—as if
we had been spun around. The address my mother clutched
led us to an entrance a few steps below street level. I remember
the corroded, over-flowing garbage cans lined up just outside
and the first creaky door of crisscrossed wire
we had to swing open as we waited for the woman to come.
I remember the sound of claws on floorboards
and her screamed commands. A five-second exposure,
that's all, but the image never stopped developing for me:
the huge arms, face and neck covered with oozing boils,
the stringy unwashed hair, and sweat, pungent
even through the screen. I knew the forest Grimm,
I knew the biblical tales of lepers, innocent pariahs
forced to sound an alarm wherever they went.
But we were the ones ringing the bell, and the only warning
was a growl—from a mongrel, not the beagle
that was to be my birthday gift. *No, I'm afraid...no,
we can't*, my mother grabbed my hand and backed away.
Every decade of a person's life, I think something happens
to mark you. This was it for me at ten.

Hell Gate

> —In Astoria Park, near the site of New York's
> single greatest loss of life until 9/11

We're banned down there where smashed beer bottles
    glint in green fragments across a shore-strip
of jagged black rocks. Their razor edges won't ever
    be smoothed, born again as beach glass.

Children nearby shriek in the new playground
    named Charybdis— oblivious to sea monsters
and the madman once rumored to lurk nights
    beneath the Hell Gate Bridge, luring boozy teens.

You tell me your late, wild cousins defied the shadows,
    shrugged off tales of bodies dumped
inside its cavernous chamber, and a phantom train
    that stopped to release drowned sailors' ghosts.

Here the waters roil, a whirlpool treacherous
    as the Straits of Messina. Worse, the churning
of human neglect that took nearly all the immigrants
    bound for a church picnic on the General Slocum.

This plaque recalls the disaster but omits the spreading
    cigarette spark, reported but ignored;
rotted fire hoses; life preservers spilling cork dust;
    and a captain who steamed ahead, fanning the flames.

In June 1904, did city bells toll for the dead?
Were one thousand, twenty-one names read?

As if on cue, we hear a dirge of chimes rising.
    The waves orchestrate, licking the shattered
green glass, the faint sound of a thousand bells
    repeating with every wake.

City Hawk

What does the raptor know of what lies in watch
behind the windows' glare?

Hunched on a branch in late winter,
he wears city-dwellers' dun-colored camouflage
and the hyper-vigilant look we assume,
surrounded by strangers.
From my apartment window I'm just
another pair of eyes peering out
from this enclosure, its brick façade
like fortress walls.

A hush descends over the creatures
that hop, flitter, scamper and slither
here in our block-long garden that's now
a domed sepulcher—

a hush more alarming than a sudden siren wail
until, like death's reprieve,
our predator vanishes—palpable absence
within squirrel click and sparrow peep,
all that unvanquished stirring back to life.

Speaking in Tongues

He sits across from me on the train and because
custom demands that no eyes meet, I gaze

at his feet, then the tongue of his left, thrust shoe—
a worker's heavy, sturdy shoe with its thick, stiff tongue

rising high from frayed and splattered laces, the tongue
that must make way each morning for the calloused foot,

and pushed back unpaid-overtime-hours later
to release the swollen foot. The tongue

that lies close to cement, steel beams, the earth,
above the worn-down sole that lives even closer.

When the doors open at the factory stop,
another man enters, and he too wears battered,

dusty boots. But his are restless, tapping and grinding
into the floor as if the machine still lived within.

The Blank Billboard

Its whiteness

    on the subway tile

in this tangled wood

a welcome abyss

        to stop by on this snowy evening

and linger before the roaring

        comes to take me.

The framed blankness

a word-less space

        and image-less,

but crowded on all sides

        by advertisements.

Alone

    at the end of the platform,

I squint and stare

        as if at the white

of my eye magnified

    through crosshairs.

Snow Has Taped Shut the Loud Mouth of My City

crept in like a bandit
from a mountain hideout
to muffle the storm of sirens,
the noisy, driving wind
of our ambition.

The city struggles:
shovels scrape concrete
like the nails of a prisoner,
desperate wheels
spin into stasis.

Each random thought falls,
one onto another,
accruing depth and heft.
Ideas take the shape of ice crystals,
pure form, irrefutable.

Later, the meltdown:
all brilliance vanished
in the pool of forgetting.

Four:

Her Secrets

Miss Revlon

My brother rescued her
from the toy factory fire, lifted her
from ashes on the sidewalk where she lay
with a platoon of melted soldiers
and warped pickup trucks.

She lay in her seamed stockings
and one gooey, high-heeled shoe
under the shriek and slanted light
of the elevated train,
where today men promise *chica*,
pushing photo cards
into the hands of other men.

I shampooed the cinders
from her smoky blonde hair,
wiped from her face
the smudged tracks of hosed char
that mimicked a woman's tears.

But her sly smile told me
she'd never cry, even if she could,
despite the trauma of her close escape—
a Scarlet O'Hara
years before I watched the epic
with my high school friends,
wanting to be that kind of survivor,
clueless about the war ahead.

Handbag

Strap grafted onto her forearm, it swung
like a clock's pendulum as my mother
walked or, more precisely, strode farther
and faster than anyone else. She belonged
to herself alone, and marked time
to that swing and jangle within, bag locked
with the sound of a vault closing to block
marauders. Hijab, blanket, bank, anodyne,
purse to heart-clutch or cradle, slab of black
leather impenetrable, secret mother lode
unreachable, protector of the code
unbreakable. Yet when I fell and cracked
my skull, she ran to me—it flew from her grip
and lay abandoned by a wall, mouth agape.

The Children's Wing

Not a place to take flight but where downy-skinned
children can sometimes heal like fallen sparrows

in a shoe box, a place I found myself at nine,
concussed.   The child in the rail-rimmed bed

was crying out in the night,
his stuffed toy fallen beyond reach,

and pretending to sleep, I felt his bottomless sorrow
as my own.   *Please pick it up*

over and over begged the child of perhaps four years,
a cry unheard until the nurse arrived

at last. Not his mother, I thought, but surely
like her. Instead a woman

who bent over the boy, growling
Shut up, shut up or I'll give you the needle

until his pleas ended with a whimper,
O.K., but can you pick it up?—

a scene that knocked my view of the world
askew. Suddenly I was bereft—of what

exactly, I didn't know, but crushed
by inexpressible loss.   Poor dumb witness.

Comic Book Man

We were children peering
        into darkness in daylight
                peering into the basement window
watching the man.

He was skinny & shirtless,
        sprawled across a bare cot,
                up to his thighs in a crazy quilt
of comic books.

They were strewn across the cement floor,
        blanketing his cell:
                one paint-chipped chair,
an empty wall hook, a hot plate.

We were children peering
        at the man who lolled
                on a bare mattress,
his soles inked blue,

mouth slack, eyes popping
        at comics we'd never seen.
                Never speaking
of what we witnessed, we crouched

to the side of that grimy casement,
        peering,
                each shivering
alone inside her secret.

The Classification Unit

The desk stretched before me
like a field for official landings.
A teen on her first summer job,
I felt as old as any functionary

who squinted behind a thick glass door,
awaiting the command
of documents' thud, processing
job descriptions into sour paste,

lowering my hair to make a curtain,
as if this gesture could shield me
from the despair of my office-mates:
the former Gospel singer

who'd lost her faith and hummed
sad pop tunes to the chime
of her typewriter bell,
and the would-be actress

who'd abandoned auditions
long before, lips moving silently
as she typed her given lines
onto forms with no ending.

Locks

The playground gate creaks
as it does in film noir,
catching my finger in the slide-bolt.

In shocked pain, I breathe
the smell of old metal on my skin,
and I'm a child again, finding
on the sidewalk a box filled with keys.

The container was mystery enough:
midnight blue suede, silver-stamped
like a starry sky. And those keys—
some numbered but most unmarked,
shaped for doors and other places
of adult concealment.

I inspected each one, wondering
who could lose such treasure, the entry
to chamber on chamber of secret selves.

In the playground, the children shriek
beyond the bench I share. Hunched
over her phone, the woman
beside me softly curses, and then sighs.
When her child approaches, she turns
the screen to black, locking the door.

Mother's Confession

She'd sneak into the converted stable
next to her Harlem tenement and pilfer
from the merchants' pushcarts parked there
overnight. She was about five, she said,
but knew it was wrong to root beneath
the wagons' blankets, as she rummages now
through flea market jumble, searching.

Augustine confessed in Book 2
"the excitement of thieving"
when he stole a neighbor's pears
"though attractive in neither color nor taste."

My mother never cared about pears
in pushcarts or kitchens, only the thrill
of quarry seized, the quest
for hidden treasure.

She confessed in an ER corridor
bathed in white florescence where we waited
for x-rays after another fall. And again
after her wrist shattered and later,
when two ribs cracked.

Always she and I alone
in a scrubbed passage of closed doors,
sealed in the limbo of pre-dawn,
stretchers wheeling in and out of rooms,
me looking away to listen and nod
in the Name of the Mother,
she rueful but grinning in her pain.

Erased

I	was 21.
I	was in my first post-college job.
I	had long, straight hair
	then, only then.
I	worked downtown when it was
	still seedy.
I	left the office at 5 pm.
I	was on an empty street,
	heading home.
	It was summer.
	Summer was in me.
	My new husband was in me.
I	would soon be home.
I	saw the man coming.
He	was lurching,
	reached out,
	grabbed hard between my legs.
	I shook.
	Alone on that street.
	Rooted in concrete.
Not	able to speak.
Not.	
Not	I.
Just Not.	
No,	that didn't happen.
Not	to me.
Not	me anymore.
Not	I.
Nil.	
Nada.	
No-	thing.

Young Heritage, Inc.

I swept 'round the garment factory showroom,
stopping before each buyer who fingered
the nubby wool coat I wore, appraising
up and down, inspecting the row
of brass buttons that divided me in two,
assessing the go-go swing of hem.

In a *Twilight Zone* episode I later recalled,
store mannequins took turns
becoming human, but only briefly.

Slumped on the floor of the curtained,
chairless cubicle between buyers' visits,
I felt disjointed by the alien woodenness
of my teenaged body, the rigid, painted lips
that would soon come to life when called.

Consider Her Green Dress

Begin with the sweetheart neckline,
that modest dip above the breasts, the sweep
of emerald velvet settling oh-so-slightly off shoulder,
fabric dyed to the shade of eternal burgeoning.

Note the band of silk net meant to caress
the clavicle, a dress both suggestive and proper—
a paradox like my mother, now 95,
who once yearned to be a dancer or a nun.

Admire the tiny waist cinched to highlight
the flaring skirt and that hint of danger
in three-quarter sleeves stitched to arrow points.

Now think of it as you would a theater curtain
in the thrilling moment before it rises
onto a life you watch unfold—

a dress I saw her wear only in black and white,
posed with my father in a nightclub nook
for a photographer selling memories
of their one-time married "date,"

a dress that hung plastic-embalmed in her closet
and years later, mine, a dress
once too large for me and then too small,

by then its flesh-colored netting
moth-hole-riddled,
a dress moving backwards in time,
silk returning to worm.

The Notebooks

Too many. And too many undated. Some large, their covers psychedelically swirled, with metal spirals taking me round and round into mad descent. Metal spirals like prison bars I flung myself against, spirals like Slinkys with a mind of their own undulating down steps. Some serious, black-marble-hard, so dangerous you might crack your head opening those covers. Notebooks divided for school subjects, those divisions ignored, full of faint pencil scrawls. No way to know which thought came first. Scraps of lyrics, phrases overheard, ossified kernels of ideas, first lines thwarted by margins and miasma. No *Golden Notebook* here, the title bringing back a summer when that novel was grafted onto my hands, filled my brain, the character's life held between the covers of black, red, yellow, blue and the strived-for gold. No way to know what had happened in *my* life, all sequence missing. Here and there the threads of dreams that pull me into what could feel more real than my diary: horror of slow blood-letting in a stark white room, but also flying past buildings and marveling at gargoyles too high to glimpse from pavement. Gone the wings, gone the girl.

Five:

No Known Coordinates

The Cage

—Inspired by Haruki Murakami's short story "Kino"

It was a story about a man who drifts
through his life, not feeling deeply, even when
he returns home to find his wife atop his friend.
It was about exiting silently—from the room, his job,
that particular life. I was on the subway, bent over
the page, aware of the sudden presence of a man
gripping the overhead bar. He was a giant
engulfing me like a Redwood, but I didn't look up,
eyes fixed only on the words.

It was a story I'd never read, but somehow knew.
At my stop, I hovered near the station wall
in dreary light, reading without glasses,
but seeing clearly. The man finds a new life
opening a side-street bar where jazz rules.
There is a woman who reveals
her bruises in his upstairs room, then pretends
not to know him, and the mystery of the silent man
who sits for hours, reading. Then snakes appear,
and then more, encircling his place.

I didn't look up when the platform exit-cage
spun violently—each passenger spewing
forth from his tiny cage-within-a-cage. More snakes
appear: the mysterious customer commands the man
to close and move from city to city, mailing back blank
postcards. He obeys. Something unnamed follows him
to a cheap hotel, where he hunkers down to watch TV
and read the faces of office workers across the way.

There is a knocking on his door in the night;
a day later, a knocking outside his window
ten flights up. I may be late for where I'm headed.
Now more people are turning the cage, leaving the cage—
a whirring, human blur. I stay bent
over the page even when the words begin to merge:
This is a story I know.

Hall of Mirrors

I keep thinking about Versailles and its famous
mirrored hall where once I briefly passed, a version
of myself infinitely multiplied, and how they say
that mirrors don't lie. But since when is a reversal
accurate? Reflections of gold rococo settees don't matter,
but faces that smile or stare back from glass?
They can't be trusted. Whether white-powdered courtesans
in puffed satin or those in gel-spiked tufts and bare skin
obscured by blue runes—none of that
is what you really see. A mirror's truth:
Left is right/right is left, a kind of "War is peace/peace is war"
Newspeak. It's all about the light and how it bounces back,
blinding our eyes with its dazzling falsities.
Like the glass-glitter of shattered stars on a winter night.
Or the cold green and blue that blink at me
from my home office when I sit in the dark
at 2 am, joining their silent sentry, wondering about
sinister intent beneath the show of security,
trying to figure out if left is right and right, left.

Your blood was no longer on the stone

under the tree when I returned to the scene today,
which didn't surprise me after last night's rain.

But still I wanted to go back to see for myself,
alone this time, no longer within the circle

of five Good Samaritans, their cell phones pulled
from pockets and bags, that calloused hand

outstretched to lift you up, the young Honduran
woman who insisted on walking us to our door,

her arm linked through yours on one side,
mine grasping the other—a kindness that washed

over us like the blessing of a downpour
after searing heat. I knelt again before that tree,

under its budding leaves, that bloodied stone
unstained now, pale gray on its patch of earth,

oddly grateful for the wound that brought strangers
to us, and me to you as you lay, later, on our bed.

When I emailed the person who'd escorted us home,
offering my thanks again—coffee or lunch

if she had the time—she didn't reply. She'd vanished
into our neighborhood of immigrants,

most ignored by longtime residents like us,
some praised, others maligned.

"Angels act, then disappear," Father Santo said
when I told our story, a smile crossing his face,

and I wondered if priests speak of angels with irony.
But I know this person in her white high-tops

walks and falls to the same earth we do, this stranger
who wanted no thanks, nameless and numinous.

Rain

—A 1919 "cine poem" by Joris Ivens filmed in Amsterdam

Seized by silent motion on a side wall,
seized by that rain that time that place:
museum-goers eddy around me.
I'm in a palm raised to feel the first drop,
windows cranked shut by unseen hands,
shades flapping. Bare trees on a bank
shift their branches, waving upside down
on the surface of a canal, and I'm spun around,
forgetting the year and season. I've ducked
under a huge black umbrella,
its ribs a span of arches,
safe as a refugee in a medieval cloister.
I'm looking down on a horse stamping
the weather, joined the crowds to board a trolley,
my cloche tugged tighter against the wind. Now
I ride past the cobblestone streets, wet streaks
jittery against the windowpane. Abandoned
wash sags on a line, barrels overflow,
a marble statue drips water like sweat
from his stone body, drain pipes gush
torrents that enter into the street's river.

Jumping off the trolley, I trail behind
three schoolgirls in tandem, heads hooded
with wool coats, a six-legged being in motion, while
small white birds rise as one from a slick rail.
When I dive into reflections, I feel most alive:
the puddle where a poodle strains
against his leash and oxfords hurry by,
then vanish; the shiny black fender that captures,
for a second, an umbrella sailing past.

High up, the first splashes of light filter downward
through iron girders crisscrossing the sky.
Stillness descends. In the canal,
rain-drop circles no longer quiver and multiply.

*

Where is that black-and-white photo of myself
in a long dark dress someone from that time
once wore, that decades-old photo of a young woman
who peers out from behind the mirrored door
of our turn-of-the-century armoire?

Where has it gone? And she? I'm there in 1919,
I'm here, a shivery-cold day in New York City,
first month of another new year,
nearly one hundred gone since that rain,
and still I find myself inside the curved vault
of a silk umbrella, watching one crystal bead
cling to a spoke, and how it holds within itself
what light the rain allows.

Film Loop: Two Hotels

Memories that may be dreams:
There I am, a young woman, maybe
thirty, floating alone in a pool.
Florida, I think.
Dusk, I think.
Medusa-haired mermaids
on tile shimmying to escape.
Empty deck chairs,
a lizard crawling by a cloudy glass
abandoned to cracked concrete.

Like someone in "Last Year at Marienbad,"
I wonder: Was I there before?

*

A nineteenth-century hotel that lists
on a bluff, slanted floors tipping us into
the Atlantic: airless tomb
in summer heat, doors opened wide
to couples sitting on beds
back-to-back in darkness.

Did I kick to the Charleston
on that portico, sip bootlegged Champagne,
lean against the now-crumbling columns,
inhaling spindrift?

Is my photo from a hundred years ago nailed
within its labyrinth of corridors?

Scratching the Surface

Needle scraped against my small, bare sole.

Feel this?

Yes, the sting is a good thing,
that holding on to pain's sensation
after strike of skull on pavement.

Do you remember?

Yes, it's one memory that clings
in this life where sting lies in wait.

Do you feel nothing else?

Sometimes, heat—this sun
penetrating epidermis of T-shirt—call it
      an embrace.

What's hard is to break
      the glamorous, deceptive veneer
to unseal what you can't name,
      but sense that you need. Begin

with these tree branch shadows
      that skim across the grass and meet,
tipping their wide-brimmed hats,
      and the birds that dive and graze
the bending blades, then vanish.

Beside me, you're reading an article
      on chaos theory,
looking up to say,

No predictions can ever be counted on
because of what we now don't see or know.

Message to Google Earth

Banded with a paper bracelet, my wrist
now bears my name, D.O.B.,
double-decked numbers and a bar code.

Google Earth, I'm here—in a medical high-rise,
down from First Avenue, across
the street from Bed Bath & Beyond, in view
of the bridge that spans the East River.
Millions of dwellings lie on both sides,
but resist the urge to track them. Instead,

pull like a magnet towards my bar code
and arrive on the 9th floor, in the outer waiting
room. I hear my name; follow me
into the undressing cubicle, then the inner hub
where the gowned women wait,
paper bracelets shifting as fingers tap phones,
our communal dance
performed in place, eyes cast down.

Trace my passage into the ice locker
with its whirring machine and vice-grip,
back to the hall and into that dim
fluorescent room of trapped twilight. Hover near
as the sticky magic wand tracks
the body's tundra across a screen.

Follow the white-robed tech
as she exits, but focus back on me.
Now stop.
Enlarge the image to woman lying on her back
in that last waiting room:
land of no known coordinates.

Of Tattoos and Medieval Messages

Julian of Norwich promised: *All shall be well*
and all shall be well, a belief the mystic
wrote and spoke when counseling seekers from her cell
with its small open window. I want that faith, but the cynic
in me rebels against the serenely unfazed. How
could she be sure with famine and bubonic plague
ravaging more than half her city? How
could she imagine a maternal God and be unafraid
to avow such odd ideas? Then I'm sent an online image:
Julian's mantra blue-inked across the back
of a modern young woman, an ancient message
in the flesh that pierces me through the straightjacket
I've worn in my own hermitage this disastrous year.
I will try, I will try, to love and live without fear.

The Parking Lot

The underground kind is where crimes
occur in the films we watch—a lone woman,
a man gunning the gas, a sudden knife.
But I don't mean that kind of place.

I'm talking instead about life lost
above ground. The desolation of waking
to a smear of rain drops that course
down a chain hotel window, and below,

rows of SUVs in a blackened sea. I'm talking
about parking lots unfathomable as ocean.
Once visiting another state, we walked
along a narrow path to a church. You left

me there that Sunday—a vast, balconied space
where altar servers were beamed onto screens
like a Multiplex theater without stained glass.
When the doors opened, the worshippers

quickly vanished, like spirits, into their cars.
You found me standing outside alone,
and together we searched in vain as we sparred
over where to find the trailhead back,

circling and crossing from one vacant
lot to the next—just you and I in that desert.

Two Meetings

—At P.S. 1, Museum of Modern Art

I'm feeling very bourgeois because I'm here but unpierced
except for my earlobes which don't count, and instead
of big black Buddy Holly glasses that all the museum interns
are sporting with such aplomb, I'm wearing contacts,
which, let's face it, are just a common cover up for common
myopia, the opposite of making a bold statement.

Upstairs I come upon a closed door in a long hall
of doors opening to exhibits, but there's a sign outside
inviting all to join the "meeting." Sudden cold
blast on my skin. High-backed pews line the empty
space that could be a Quaker hall. I take my place, add
my eyes to the four pairs fixed on wispy clouds
drifting across today's very blue sky, open-air
and framed for viewing. Disembodied male voice:
"Thanks for coming to the meeting." She,
also disembodied, enthuses, "Isn't this the neatest thing?"
I tip-toe out, and elevator down

to the unfinished basement, a warren of cluttered
cubicles, passing through an unmarked door
like Alice, and finding myself alone in another hall.
Only one open door: I gingerly descend makeshift
plywood steps even lower, flanked on both sides
by oddly gilded boilers beneath a ceiling that presses in.
A noose huge enough for a slave ship spreads
across the dank floor, weave of thick iron chains
and frayed, filthy rope, ugly as history.
When I turn to go, I hear behind me what sounds
like a trap door banging open and shut.
I don't stop to look or count the bodies.

Galilee

—The largest commercial fishing port in Rhode Island

My friend Carla has brought me
to this port of sagging piers
cracked like the faces of fishermen.

Rust eats the hulls of small boats,
but not enough to corrode the hope
of those who cast off pre-dawn
in depleted waters, a faith that seems
to persist like my prayers drowsily mumbled
into the void of another morning.

Spools bulge with line and netting
on massive ships built to spend weeks
at sea watching for signs.
But at dusk in Galilee, all is stasis,
decks and docks forsaken.

I fight this feeling of emptiness and waiting
and think of my mother—homebound,
nearly blind, half-deaf, broken-hipped,
wanting, needing.

Yes, I'm asking for miracles—
the scraps and crumbs
of my daily portion multiplied
to plenty, storms calmed with a word,
a hand outstretched if I'm drowning.

Carla breaks my reverie, points out
the Harbor of Refuge, a four-mile breakwater
on the horizon—built to save lives, she says—
and to our right, Jerusalem.

On New Year's Eve

A sky at first remote,

then gone, as if even a modest idea

of heaven—sunset's thumbprint pressed

to half-closed eyes—were out of reach.

Lately I live like a sleepwalker

but one born under a lucky sign

who misses walls, stretched wires,

steep stairs that appear without warning.

Dramatic ends demand awareness—

what good is the tragic hero asleep?

And so I'm content to stumble

through fog this New Year's Eve, believing

that a shift will come, a star, a kiss.

About the Author

Maria Terrone is the author of three previous full-length collections: *The Bodies We Were Loaned* (The Word Works, 2002), *A Secret Room in Fall*, winner of the McGovern Prize (Ashland Poetry Press, 2006), *Eye to Eye* (Bordighera Press, 2014), and two chapbooks: *American Gothic, Take 2* (Finishing Line Press, 2009) and *Life, Death & Cash* (Dancing Girl Press, 2024). Her poetry, which has been published in French and Farsi, has appeared in such media as *Poetry*, *Ploughshares*, *The Hudson Review*, *Poetry Daily*, and Verse Daily, and read on National Public Radio. Her first-place awards include the Elinor Benedict Prize in Poetry (*Passages North*), Allen Tate Memorial Award (*Wind*), and the Mathiasen Award (*Harmony*, published by the medical humanities program at the University of Arizona College of Medicine).

Her poems have also appeared in more than 30 anthologies from publishers including Alfred A. Knopf, CavanKerry Press, The Feminist Press, and Beacon Press. In 2015, she became poetry editor of the scholarly and creative journal *Italian Americana*. As a long-time contributor to *The Hudson Review* (Paula Deitz, editor), she has happily participated in its Writers in the Schools program. She is also author of *At Home in the New World* (Bordighera Press, 2018), creative nonfiction essays. A native New Yorker, she lives with her husband in Jackson Heights, Queens, and enjoys her extra time for the arts after a career in corporate and university communications.

For more information, please visit mariaterrone.com.

About The Word Works

Since its founding in 1974, The Word Works has steadily published volumes of contemporary poetry and presented public programs. Its imprints include The Washington Prize, The Tenth Gate Prize, The Hilary Tham Capital Collection, and International Editions.

Monthly, The Word Works offers free programs in its Café Muse Literary Salon. Starting in 2023, the winners of the Jacklyn Potter Young Poets Competition will be presented in the June Café Muse program.

As a 501(c)3 organization, The Word Works has received awards from the National Endowment for the Arts, the National Endowment for the Humanities, the D.C. Commission on the Arts & Humanities, the Witter Bynner Foundation, Poets & Writers, The Writer's Center, Bell Atlantic, the David G. Taft Foundation, and others, including many generous private patrons.

An archive of artistic and administrative materials in the Washington Writing Archive is housed in the George Washington University Gelman Library. The Word Works is a member of the Community of Literary Magazines and Presses.

wordworksbooks.org

Other Word Works Books

Annik Adey-Babinski, *Okay Cool No Smoking Love Pony*
Emily August, *The Punishments Must Be a School*
Jennifer Barber, *The Sliding Boat Our Bodies Made*
Rachel Bennett: *Mothers & Other Fairy Tales*
Andrea Carter Brown, *September 12*
Willa Carroll, *Nerve Chorus*
Grace Cavalieri, *Creature Comforts / The Long Game: Poems Selected & New*
Abby Chew, *A Bear Approaches From the Sky*
Nadia Colburn, *The High Shelf*
Henry Crawford, *The Binary Planet*
Barbara Goldberg, *Berta Broadfoot and Pepin the Short
    / Breaking & Entering: New and Selected Poems*
Akua Lezli Hope, *Them Gone*
Michael Klein, *The Early Minutes of Without: Poems Selected & New*
Deborah Kuan, *Women on the Moon*
Frannie Lindsay, *If Mercy*
Elaine Magarrell, *The Madness of Chefs*
Chloe Martinez, *Ten Thousand Selves*
Marilyn McCabe, *Glass Factory*
JoAnne McFarland, *Identifying the Body*
Leslie McGrath, *Feminists Are Passing From Our Lives*
Kevin McLellan, *Ornitheology*
Ron Mohring, *The Boy Who Reads in the Trees*
A. Molotkov, *Future Symptoms*
Ann Pelletier, *Letter That Never*
W. T. Pfefferle, *My Coolest Shirt*
Ayaz Pirani, *Happy You Are Here*
Robert Sargent, *Aspects of a Southern Story / A Woman From Memphis*
Roger Smith, *Radiation Machine Gun Funk*
Jeddie Sophronius, *Love & Sambal*
Julia Story, *Spinster for Hire*
Barbara Ungar, *After Naming the Animals*
Cheryl Clark Vermeulen, *They Can Take It Out*
Julie Marie Wade, *Skirted*
Miles Waggener, *Superstition Freeway*
Fritz Ward, *Tsunami Diorama*
Camille-Yvette Welsch, *The Four Ugliest Children in Christendom*
Amber West, *Hen & God*
Maceo Whitaker, *Narco Farm*